I0117725

William Cecil Dabney

# The Value of Chemistry to the Medical Practitioner

a dissertation to which was awarded the Boylston Prize, June 5th, 1873

William Cecil Dabney

**The Value of Chemistry to the Medical Practitioner**
*a dissertation to which was awarded the Boylston Prize, June 5th, 1873*

ISBN/EAN: 9783337816353

Printed in Europe, USA, Canada, Australia, Japan

Cover: Foto ©Andreas Hilbeck / pixelio.de

More available books at **www.hansebooks.com**

# THE

# VALUE OF CHEMISTRY

TO THE

# MEDICAL PRACTITIONER.

———— • ◆ • ————

A DISSERTATION TO WHICH WAS AWARDED
THE BOYLSTON PRIZE, JUNE 5TH, 1873.

## BY WM. C. DABNEY, M. D.

CHARLOTTESVILLE:
CHRONICLE STEAM BOOK AND JOB PRINTING HOUSE,
1873.

# PREFACE.

The Boylston Prize Committee proposed two questions for the year 1873. One on "Electro Therapeutics," and the other on "The Value of Chemistry to the Medical Practitioner."

The following essay is an answer to the second of these questions; and it is now published by the author for distribution among his friends, with the hope that they may find here, in a condensed form, some information which they could not otherwise obtain, except by an amount of reading and study for which but few physicians in active practice have the time.

" By an order adopted in 1826 the secretary (of the Boylston Prize Committee) was directed to publish annually the following votes :

"1st. That the Board do not not consider themselves as approving the doctrines contained in any of the dissertations to which premiums may be adjudged.

"2d. That in case of publication of a successful dissertation the author to consider as bound to print the above vote in connection therewith."

# The Value of Chemistry to the Medical Practitioner.

That a knowledge of chemistry is of essential service to the medical practitioner will scarcely be denied at the present day. So far as we are informed, Mr. Samuel Wilks is the only physician of any eminence who does not believe in a rational system of therapeutics.

(Lancet, January 18th, 1871.)

In the present state of pathology we cannot say that *all* diseases are owing to chemical changes in the solids or fluids of the organism; nor are we in a position to affirm that all medicines act chemically in the relief or cure of disease. *Many* diseases, however, are certainly owing to chemical changes, and in those diseases medicines are generally given which are expected to act chemically for their relief.

It frequently happens that there are various morbid conditions at the same time in the same individual, some of which seem to be owing to chemical changes, while others, so far as we know at present, have no direct connection with such changes.

In treating of such morbid conditions in the ensuing pages, we shall only speak of those which chemistry teaches us, or for the relief or cure of which chemical means are used. Some of the chemical theories of disease have been shown by experiment and clinical experience to be correct ; others are as yet only suppositions. We shall endeavor, so far as it is possible, to draw a line between those which *have* and those which have *not* been proven.

A general statement of the different uses of chemistry to

the medical practitioner will enable us afterwards to prosecute our studies to better advantage.

I have attempted, under the following six headings, to state these uses *generally.*

Chemistry is of use to the medical practitioner—

1. In teaching him the chemical composition of the different solids and fluids of the organism, and the various chemical changes which take place in the body in health.

2. In teaching him the chemical changes which take place in disease, and in furnishing him with the means of detecting such changes.

3. In teaching him the action of medicines in the system on the chemical components of the body, and the action of medicines on each other.

4. In furnishing him with the means of counteracting improper chemical changes in the system.

5. In the detection of poisons and in teaching the manner of counteracting them.

6. In teaching the composition of and detecting adulterations in articles of diet, in medicines, &c.

It is plain that it would be inconvenient to consider our subject in the order that it is stated in the above general headings. We propose to consider—

1. The different fluids of the organism.

2. The different solids of the organism.

3. The chemical tests for the different poisons and their antidotes.

4. Those substances which are chemically incompatible.

The chemical composition and the uses of the different kinds of food, medicines and mineral waters will be considered in considering the different diseased states.

In considering both the fluids and solids we shall study—First, briefly, their physiological chemistry; secondly, their pathological chemistry; and, thirdly, the therapeutical indications to which their pathological chemistry gives rise, and the means of fulfilling them. The necessity of a correct knowledge of the physiology of an organ before we can understand its pathology is universally admitted; and hence we need make no explanation for pursuing our studies in the order stated above.

The fluids of the organism are:

*Secretions.*—Blood, mucus, milk, tears, sebaceous matter, (semi-solid), saliva, gastric juice, pancreatic juice, bile, serum of serous, membrane, perspiration.

*Excretions.*—Urine.

Bile may be classed under both headings (secretions and excretions), for the general opinion among physiologists at the present day is that the liver is both an excreting and secreting organ—excreting cholesterine and secreting sugar.

It frequently happens that the presence of some abnormal ingredient in one of the fluids is accompanied by its absence or presence in reduced quantity in some other where it normally belongs. For example—when urea is present in large quantity in the blood, it is absent or present in greatly reduced quantity in the urine.

In such cases the pathological condition will be considered at length under one of the fluids, and briefly considered under the other.

### BLOOD.

The blood, circulating as it does through the entire body, carrying nourishment to the various parts of the body and absorbing the effete materials, which in their turn are to be eliminated from it by the appropriate organs, must necessarily be intimately associated with many of the "ills which flesh is heir to." At the present day, however, it is rarely examined chemically in disease. One reason for this, perhaps, is that bloodletting, as a remedy, is much more rarely resorted to now than formerly. For our knowledge of the chemical constitution of the blood in the different diseases we are chiefly indebted to Simon. Before considering the chemical changes in diseases, however, we should have a cor-

rect understanding of the chemical composition of the blood
in health.

Its physical characters are too well known to need a word
of explanation ; nor does it belong properly to the subject
under consideration. Becquerel and Rodier give the following table (taken from
Flint's Physiology of Man, Vol. 1, p. 132), as showing the
mean result of the analysis of the blood of twenty-two healthy
men :

[Becquerel and Rodier's table showing the composition of the blood.]

| | | |
|---|---|---|
| Density of the blood, | - - - | 1050.000 |
| Water, - - - - - - | | 881.600 |
| Globulin, - - - - | | 135.000 |
| Albumen, - - - - - | | 70.000 |
| Fibrin, - - - . - | | 2.500 |
| Seroline, - - - - - | | 0.025 |
| Cholesterine, - - - - - | | 0.126 |
| Carbonate of Soda, Free Soda, Sulphate of Soda, Phosphate of Soda, Carbonate of Potash, Sulphate of Potash, Phosphate of Potash, Sulphate of Magnesia, | Carbonate of soda most abundant, - | 2.300 |
| Phosphate of Lime, Phosphate of Magnesia, | - - - | 0.350 |
| Iron, - - - - - | | 0.550 |
| Undetermined extractive matters, | - - | 2.450 |

Besides the substances given in the above table and the
gases contained in the blood, the following have been found
to be either constant or temporary constituents :

Sugar, in the hepatic veins.

Fatty emulsion, in small quantity after eating.

Coloring matter of the serum.

Urea, in very minute quantities.

Uric acid (as urate of soda) in minute quantity.

Creatine and creatinine, in small quantity.

Having thus briefly considered the physiological chemistry of the blood, we shall proceed to study—

1. The increase or decrease of the normal constituents of the blood; their clinical significance, and the therapeutical indications derived from them; and

2. The presence of foreign matters in the blood, their clinical significance, &c.

————

1. Plethora.—An increase in the solid constituents of the blood, particularly the red corpuscles, constitutes plethora. But little is known concerning the formation of the red corpuscles, and hence we can do nothing *directly* to lessen their formation. Bearing in mind their chemical composition we may do something by the administration of suitable diet, but even this is very unsatisfactory. Certain medicines, such as mercury, seem to have the power of lessening the number of red globules. The *manner* in which they do this is unknown. Mr. Odling, in his animal chemistry, pp. 146–156, (London edition,) advances a theory concerning the *modus operandi* of alteratives, which gives a possible clue to the action of mercury in lessening the number of red corpuscles. His theory is that mercury, iodine, arsenic, and other medicines act by virtue of their "chemical mobility," or by their power of deoxidizing when there is an excess of oxygen, and oxidizing when oxygen is wanted. This theory is certainly plausible, but, of course, it is as yet *only* a theory. Every one, however, is familiar with the use of the *proto*-salts of mercury, arsenic, &c., in the laboratory, as *de*-oxidizing agents, and the use of the *per*-salts of the same metals as *oxidizing* agents, and we can see no reason why these substances should not have the same action on the constituents of the human body.

2. Anaemia.—A decrease in the number of red blood corpuscles constitutes Anaemia.

The whole volume of blood is frequently reduced by hemorrhage, but the watery portion is quickly replaced by absorp-

2

tion. The red corpuscles have been known, however, to become as low as 70, 60, or even 21 parts per 1,000, (*Flint's Physiology, p.* 61.)

Anaemia occurs in tuberculosis, cancer, Bright's disease, hemorrhages, affections of the liver—especially cirrhosis—all febrile disorders, malaria, saturnine diseases as a result of the administration of mercury and chlorosis.—(*Flint*).

The therapeutical indications are to furnish food rich in albumen and the administration of iron.—(*Headland on action of remedies in the system, pp.* 319–320). Let us, therefore, consider briefly the articles of diet which are most suitable from their chemical composition to restore the lost elements to the blood. In the first place we should bear in mind that all the nitrogenized alimentary principles are converted into albumen before they are applied to the nutrition of the tissues. The fluid form of albumen is most easily digested, then coagulated albumen, then fibrin, then casein, and lastly the derivatives of albumen, gelatine, chondrine and cartilage.—(*Letheby on Food, p.* 55). Skim cheese contains by far the largest per cent. of nitrogenous matters (44.8 per cent.), but this is in the form of casein, and we have already seen that this is not very digestible. Lean beef contains about 19 per cent. Mutton a little less. The nitrogenized matters in the meats are, of course, in the form of fibrin. Eggs, which contain albumen in a liquid form and hence in the most digestible condition, contain 14 per cent. The quantity of nitrogenized materials in the different articles of food given above is taken from Letheby.—(Table 3, p. 5). Other chemists differ with him slightly. Berzelius found that the flesh of the ox contained about 2.20 per cent. of albumen analogous to the white of egg and the serum of the blood, and Payen found about 22.93 per cent. of nitrogenized matters in cooked beefsteak. The same author found 4.30 per cent. of nitrogenized matters in cow's milk. Besides the large quantity of albumen contained in eggs, *iron* is also found in the ash after incineration. The vegetables containing albumen (or substances convertible into it), in most common use, are wheat, which contains from 13 to 15 per cent. of gluten ; the succulent vegetables which contain vegetable albumen are peas, beans, &c., which contain a substance analogous to casein.

Of course, in the selection of articles of diet for sick persons, care should be taken to choose those which, besides having a suitable chemical composition, are most easy of digestion.

Iron, which, as we have seen in the table given previously, exists in the blood in the proportion of 0.550 per 1,000, is found in the hematine or coloring matter of the blood ; and hence when the globules are lessened in amount the quantity of iron is also lessened. It should, therefore, be supplied in some form as the food we take does not contain it in sufficient quantity to supply the loss. The form or particular preparation of iron used does not seem to be a matter of much consequence. Dr. C. D. Meigs, it is true, recommended the pure iron (iron by hydrogen), on chemical grounds, because he thought that the simple action of the acids of the stomach upon the metal would require a less expenditure of force than if a salt of iron had to be decomposed, and then acted upon in such a way as to be absorbed by the stomach and intestines. Those who believe that the acidity of the gastric juice is caused by hydrochloric acid will probably think that it is owing to this fact that the muriated tincture of iron seems, in many cases, to be preferable to the other preparations. The supporters of the lactic acid theory of the gastric acidity might argue in a similar manner, but all of the views, although more or less plausible, are only theories, and do not admit of proof.

3. Fibrin.—Fibrin is found in the blood in the proportion of 2.50 parts per 1,000. It coagulates outside of the body, and under certain circumstances in it. It is soluble in dilute solutions of caustic alkalies and in phosphoric acid.—(*Fowne's Chemistry*, p. 544). The means by which fibrin was held in solution in the blood was for a long time unknown. Various hypothesis were advanced, but until the year 1856 no definite conclusions were reached. In that year Dr. B.W. Richardson expe-

rimented at great length upon the subject, and came to the conclusion that fibrin was held in solution in the blood by ammonia, and that it was the loss of ammonia by evaporation
which caused the fibrin to coagulate out of the body. These
views were adopted by the great majority of physiologists, and
are generally entertained at the present day. Richardson, it
is true, has withdrawn his views on the subject of the fibrin
of the blood being held in solution in that fluid by ammonia,
but the fact remains that it is soluble in ammonia and the
other alkalies. It is not necessary, however, for us to pursue
our studies further in this direction. Certain it is that chemistry has shown that fibrin is soluble in the alkalies and their
carbonates, and from this, much useful information may be
drawn by the practical physician.

HYPERINOSIS.—In certain diseased conditions the relative
amount of fibrin is increased and this increase is called by
Simon, "Hyperinosis." According to this author the following are the chief diseases in which the amount of fibrin is increased : Metro-peritonitis, carditis, bronchitis, pneumonitis,
pleuritis, nephritis, cystitis, rheumatism, erysipelas, phthisis,
puerperal fever and eclampsia. Of these, acute articular
rheumatism presents the largest increase of fibrin, pneumonitis next, and capillary bronchitis next.

Blood-letting increases the relative amount of fibrin, and
hence the liability to the formation of a heart clot after severe
hemorrhages. Dr. Meigs explains this subject very ably and
fully in his "System of Obstetrics."

As before stated, it has been found that the alkalies intro-
duced into the blood vessels, or mixed with blood after it is
drawn, impede, or may arrest, the process of coagulation.
And it has been proved that nearly all medicines (all that are
soluble) are absorbed and gain access to the blood.—(*Headland, op : cit. p.* 61, *et seq*).

The practical deductions to be drawn from these facts are,
that in all those diseased conditions, when the amount of
fibrin is increased, ammonia or some other alkali should be

administered. The benefit of alkalies in the treatment of acute articular rheumatism is universally acknowledged, and we shall have occasion, in a future section, to study their *modus operandi* at greater length. The employment of ammonia in the treatment of pneumonitis is rapidly growing in favor with the profession. In hemorrhage from wounds, or injuries of any kind, when the mouth of the bleeding vessel is to be stopped by a coagulum, alkalies would be contraindicated. I have frequently used carbonate of ammonia, however, in the treatment of uterine hemorrhages, both antepartum and post-partum, and I think with good effect. Of course, the ammonia is not given to check the hemorrhage, but to prevent the formation of an embolus or heart clot afterwards. The mouths of the bleeding vessels in uterine hemorrhages are closed by their compression between the fibres of the uterus and hence the formation of a coagulum is not so desirable. Fayrer and other surgeons in India have found the injection of ammonia into the veins of great service in cholera. Of course the immediate effect of this would be that of a powerful stimulant, but we are inclined to think that besides this effect the ammonia prevents the formation of a coagulum in the heart or pulmonary vessels, which experience teaches is a common mode of death in this disease. In thrombosis and embolism also, ammonia has been used with decided benefit. Dr. B. W. Richardson first used ammonia in these cases. He has found it very advantageous to combine iodide of potassium with it, as otherwise it produces too great a *fluidity* of the blood. It is probable that this will be more serviceable as a preventative than as a cure of embolism.

Hypinosis.—A decrease in the amount of fibrin in the blood is called by Simon *Hypinosis.* This condition is much less frequent than hyperinosis. The diseases in which it occurs according to Simon are Typhoid and every form of continued fever, varioloid, rubeola, scarlatina, intermittent fever, cerebral hemorrhage.—(*Chemistry of Man, p. p.* 235-250). Flint, however, says that it occurs in continued fevers provided they are not accompanied by acute inflammation in any part. In varioloid, he says, it is above the normal standard ; in rubeola it is normal, in scarlatina a little decreased, and it is not diminished in the intermittent fevers.—(*Practice of Medicine, pp.* 70–71).

Food rich in fibrin, such as the various meats, are indicated in this diseased condition. We have seen, previously, the amount of nitrogenized matters in the leading articles of diet. The flesh of the ox is probably the richest in nitrogenized matters.

The mineral acids have been proposed on theoretical grounds and have been found of service. It was thought that as the fibrin of the blood was kept in a fluid condition by an alkali, that if a portion of the alkali were neutralized by an acid more fibrin would accumulate. Probably a more rational explanation is, that by the administration of acids a larger amount of acid is set free in the blood, and is thus furnished to the gastric juice to aid in digestion.—(*Headland, op : cit, pp.* 121–122). If the latter theory be the correct one, it is probable that lactic acid or the acid phosphate of lime would be as serviceable as the mineral acids.

4. ALBUMEN.—Albumen is present in the blood in the proportion of 70 parts per 1,000. All the nitrogenous substances which are taken in the system as food seem to be converted into albumen before they are absorbed. Fibrin, which plays so important a part in the animal economy, is formed from albumen. It may be either increased or diminished in quantity. Concerning its increase, but little is known. It is diminished in Bright's disease of the kidneys, and in some other affections of the same organ ; and when it is present in the blood in too small quantity, it is usually present in the urine. The density of the blood is owing chiefly to albumen, and hence, when the quantity of this ingredient is diminished, the serum of the blood transudes and causes *dropsy.* This theory of the cause of dropsy, it is true, has been opposed by Dr. H. C. Wood, of Philadelphia, (*American Journal of*

*Medical Sciences, July,* 1871,) but it is generally thought that his arguments are not sufficient to overthrow it. The quantity of urea and of albumen in the blood seem to bear an inverse proportion to each other. We shall have occasion to refer to this more fully hereafter. As the *presence* of albumen in the urine is a much more prominent symptom than its absence in the blood, the subject of albuminuria can more appropriately be considered under the head of *urine.*

5. Fat.—Fat, as we have seen previously, exists in the blood after a full meal in considerable quantity. One source of the fat of the blood is that taken with the food as fat, but Claude Bernard showed that fat was produced by the liver, at the expense of the saccharine or amylaceous articles of food. The amount generated or deposited in the system may be greatly increased by a diet consisting largely of fatty or amylaceous articles and by muscular inactivity. An excess of fat in the heart is apt to coëxist with fatty degenerations of the heart or other parts of the muscular system.

The indications when it is present in abnormally large quantity, are to give food which contains as small a quantity as possible of fatty or amylaceous matter, and to make the patient take as active exercise as his strength will admit of. Nitrogenized articles of diet are suitable. A small quantity of fat will nearly always find its way into the system, but this will be burnt off in keeping up the animal heat. Corn bread should be avoided on account of the oil or fat which it contains. The bread used should be made of white well "bolted" flour. This is not nearly so fattening as corn bread. Mr. Thomas J. Hand, of New York, in a *very able* pamphlet on wheat and the process of converting it into flour, has shown that most of the gluten is removed with the bran in the manufacture of flour. A French machinist has invented a machine by which this gluten, which is the most nourishing part of the wheat, can be retained in the flour, and thus the proportion of nitrogenous matter in it greatly increased.

Lean meat should be used, particularly beef or mutton. Of

fowls only those with white meat are appropriate. The dark meat fowls have the fat and lean mixed together in such a manner that it cannot be separated. It is highly probable that mercury would lessen the quantity of fat in the system, but as far as I am aware no observations have been made on on this subject, and, indeed, when there was fatty degeneration of the heart, mercury would be contra-indicated.

6. GLUCO-HAEMIA.—Sugar is found in the blood in health in small quantity—in the hepatic veins and right side of the heart. Its function is probably to assist in the formation of fat and the production of animal heat. Its presence in the blood in abnormal quantity constitutes "*Gluco-haemia.*" It makes its appearance in the urine at the same time, and will be considered under that head on account of the facility with which it is recognized in that fluid.

7. URAEMIA.—Urea, as we have seen in the table given previously, exists in the blood in health in very minute quantity. Wartz has shown that it is present in the lymph and chyle in large quantity. In health urea is excreted by the kidney. These organs were at one time thought to produce it (Oppler). The experiments of Bernard, Barreswill, and Hammond, however, have shown that it is formed in the system by the general process of disassimilation and taken up by the blood to be separated by the kidneys.

The excess of urea in the blood gives rise to a condition known as Uraemia. This excess may be owing either to excessive formation, which occurs in Leuchaemia, or to deficient elimination, which occurs commonly in connection with albuminuria.—(*Allbut on the use of the Opthalmoscope, p.* 249). Nothing is known concerning the excessive formation of urea. It may be present in the blood from deficient elimination when there is no albumen in the urine. The existence of uraemia may be inferred whenever in connection with the symptoms of uraemic poisoning the secretion of urine is greatly diminished. The urine is also generally of low specific gravity. An analysis of the urine will of course enable the physician to detect the absence or diminution of the amount of urea with certainty.

Physiological experiment and clinical experience both show that urea is eliminated vicariously by the bowels and the skin. It is converted, however, in its passage through the alimentary canal into carbonate of ammonia, and appears in the evacuations in that form. Uraemia is chiefly to be apprehended in Bright's disease—in scarlet fever, or rather as a sequel of scarlet fever, and in all cases where the circulation through the kidneys is in any way impeded. The uraemia, which occurs sometimes during pregnancy, is caused by the pressure of the gravid uterus on the veins in the pelvis. A reviewer of different works on puerperal eclampsia, &c., in the American Journal of the Medical Sciences for April, 1871, comes to the conclusion that convulsions are not caused by the presence of urea or of carbonate of ammonia in the blood; but this statement is contrary to the views entertained by the great mass of the profession, and can scarcely be accepted without further proof.

Uraemia is nearly always accompanied by albuminuria. Bearing in mind the vicarious mode of elimination of urea, by the skin and bowels, remedies would seem to be indicated to promote the action of these organs. The practice of *greasing* the skin in scarlet fever is obviously not in accordance with scientific principles as the perspiratory function is thus greatly interfered with and one channel for the elimination of urea is cut off. Greasing was resorted to to lessen the temperature, but this can be done equally well by sponging with cold water, and in this way diaphoresis is promoted rather than checked.

8. URICAEMIA.—Uric acid exists in the blood in health in minute quantity as urate of soda. Uric acid is probably formed like urea, by the general process of disassimilation in the system, and, like urea, it is excreted in health by the kidneys. Its presence in the blood in abnormal quantity gives rise to the condition known as uricaemia, and this excess has

3

been shown by Garrod to be the cause of gout. Like urea when the amount of uric acid in the blood is increased it is diminished in the urine. Garrod found that it was considerably diminished during a paroxysm of gout, and habitually lessened in the chronic form of the disease. The concretions in and around the joints in gout consist chiefly of urate of soda which is very insoluble. The indications of treatment in gout are to give remedies to counteract chemically the excess of acid and to form some salt of uric acid more soluble than the urate of soda. The salts of potash were proposed by Garrod on theoretical grounds and have been found of very great service. About eight or ten years ago carbonate of lithia was proposed as a remedy in this affection, and according to Flint, Sr., lithia water, which is a solution of lithia in corbonated water, has been found a very useful remedy in New York. Niemeyer does not recommend alkalies, but advises the free use of acid drinks during the attacks. The kind of acid is not mentioned, but it is probably lemonade to which he alludes by acid drinks. If we are right in this supposition it is extremely probable that the lemon juice acts by the conversion of the citrate of potash which it contains into carbonate of potash and the neutralization of the uric acid by this salt. Dr. Owen Rees thought the lemon juice acted by converting the uric acid into urea, which is much more soluble than uric acid. This explanation, however, is extremely improbable.—(*For a very able exposition of the relation of urea to uric acid see Odling's Animal Chemistry, London edition, pp.* 128–129). The late Dr. Buckler, of Baltimore, proposed the phosphate of ammonia with the view of obtaining by double decomposition the phosphate of soda and the urate of ammonia, both of which salts are very soluble in water—(the latter, however, only in the presence of chloride of sodium). Benzoic acid was proposed by Ure and has been used considerably with the view of converting the uric acid into hippuric acid, which is much more soluble than the uric.

9. Cholesteraemia.—Cholesterine is found in the blood

in the proportion of 0.125 parts per 1,000. It originates in some manner, as yet not understood, in the brain and nervous system, and in health is excreted by the liver—(*See article by Flint, Jr., in American Journal of the Medical Science, October,* 1862). It is discharged with the faeces as stercorine ; if retained in the blood it gives rise to a peculiar train of poisonous symptoms to which the name of cholesteraemia has been applied. Its excretion is interfered with in all structural diseases of the liver. Many cases which are thought to be uraemic poisoning are doubtless owing to the cholesterine being retained in the blood. Cholesteraemia frequently occurs during pregnancy.—(*For a very able article on this subject, by the late Dr. R. B. Nelson, of Charlottesville, Va., see the Virginia Medical Journal for November,* 1867). It has been detected in the urine during an attack of jaundice by Gmelin.—(*Simon loc. cit., p.* 532). Although it is a non-nitrogenous product, it is possible that this is the vicarious mode of its elimination, and measures to increase the action of the kidneys would be advisable. Nothing definite is known on the subject of the treatment of cholesteramia. The mercurial preparations and podophillin have been proposed from their apparent power of promoting the action of the liver.

The foreign matters most frequently found in the blood, and which are indicative of chemical changes occuring in the organism, are—

Lactic acid, biliary matters, pus.

10. RHEUMATISM.—Lactic acid is not found in the blood in health. The lactates are frequently taken into the stomach as food ; but they are speedily converted into the carbonates before reaching the blood. *Lehman proved this by experiments on his own person.* The sugar which is formed in the liver is carried by the blood to the lungs, and is then burnt off after being converted into lactic acid.—(*Flint's Phys., 1st Vol., p.* 68). It is doubtless frequently present in the blood in small quantity, and for a short time without giv-

ing rise to any disturbance; but its presence in the blood in quantity gives rise to rheumatism. This theory of the cause of rheumatism was advanced by Prout, and at the present day is generally adopted by physicians. An English physician, Dr. B. W. Foster, has recently reported two cases (*British Med. Journal, Dec.* 23d, 1871) where lactic acid was given for the cure of diabetes; and in both cases an attack of acute articular rheumatism was brought on. The attacks came on when the acid was taken, and ceased when it was discontinued. When moderate quantities of the acid were tolerated, an increase in the dose brought on the painful inflammation of the joints.

The indication of treatment then in acute articular rheumatism, so far as the lactic acid is concerned, is the administration of alkalies to counteract chemically the acid in the blood. This is the theoretical treatment of rheumatism, and experience has proved it to be the best. The carbonates of the alkalies are generally used; and of these carbonate of potash is perhaps the most popular. Some years ago the permanganate of potash was proposed, probably from the fact that the permanganic acid is feebly united with the base.— (*Fownes' Chemistry, p.* 277). The writer, while resident physician ot the Seaman's Hospital, Baltimore, in 1868, instituted a series of experiments and observations to determine the value of this salt. The conclusion reached was, that it was uncertain and could not compare with the carbonates of potash and soda and Rochelle salts as a remedy for rheumatism. We have seen previously that lactic acid is formed in the lungs from sugar. It is unnecessary in this connection for us to consider the origin and function of sugar; it is sufficient for us to bear in mind that it is produced in the organism, and is also taken in with the food. It is important therefore to give as little sacharine food, or food easily converted into sugar, as possible. Under the head of Diabetes will be given a table of the different vegetables arranged in order according to the proportion of starch which they contain.

11. BILIARY MATTERS.—Biliary matters are frequently present in the blood, giving a yellow coloring to the skin at such times. The presence of the biliary matters is symptomatic of a variety of disorders of the liver and gall bladder, but it is a matter about which but little need be said in this connection. As a general rule when the biliary coloring matter is present in the blood it also makes its appearance in the urine, and we shall notice it under that heading.

12. PYAEMIA.—Pus in the blood constitutes a morbid affection known as *pyaemia.* It seems almost useless to refer to this diseased condition in an essay on the practical value of chemistry in medicine; but as some authorities have recently proposed a mode of treatment which seems to act chemically, I have thought it proper to notice the subject briefly. It is seldom necessary to test the blood chemically for pus. The symptoms of pyaemia are usually sufficiently well marked; ammonia, however, is usually given in chemical works as a test. Blood treated with ammonia dissolves into a clear fluid, while pus similarly treated is coagulated. Hence when there is pus in the blood we find strips of stringy substance if the blood is treated with ammonia. The microscope has also been much used as a test for pus in the blood. If, however, the views of Conheim and his disciples be correct that the pus-corpuscles are identical with the white corpuscels of the blood, the microscope will be of little value in this connection. Virchow, who does not believe in this identity of white blood corpuscles and pus-corpuscles, acknowledges that the only way of distinguishing them is by their mode of origin.—(*Cellular Pathology, p.* 188). Rindfleisch says that *most* pus-corpuscels are derived from the exudation of white corpuscles, "but the participation of epithelium cannot be excluded."—(*Pathol. Histology, p.* 111). The chemical treatment of pyaemia, to which reference has previously been made, consists in placing the patient in a carbolized atmosphere, and in the administration internally of the carbolates or sulpho carbolates. This treatment has the high

sanction of Dr. Lionel Beale and Mr. John Wood.—(*Med. Press and Circular, April* 19*th,* 1871). Carbol has the power of dissolving the pus-corpuscles, and this is doubtless its mode of action in pyaemia. This treatment would acquire still greater importance if the views entertained by some histologists that the white corpuscles have the power of proliferating after being exuded should prove to be correct.— (*Vulpian and Hayden, Gazette Hebdomadaire, No.* 7, 1870). Bill found that when much oil was present, carbol was inert, and that after its solution in oil it could not be detected by chemical tests. According to Fownes as much as one per cent. of cholesterine has been found in pus, and this being a fatty substance it is probably by combining with this that the carbol acts.

### GASES IN THE BLOOD.

Having considered the increase and decrease of the normal constituents of the blood, which are in a solid or fluid condition, and having considered the abnormal ingredients which are occasionally present in the blood, we shall proceed to consider the gases which are in it.

That oxygen is taken into the blood during inspiration, and carbonic acid is given off during expiration, is universally known. The atmosphere consists of about four-fifths nitrogen and one-fifth oxygen. The nitrogen and oxygen are probably in a state of mixture, though some chemists think they are in a state of feeble chemical combination. A proper supply of oxygen is absolutely necessary to life, and if from any cause it is not obtained by inspiration, the carbonic acid remains in the blood and causes suffocation.

13. ASTHMA.—Let us now see under what circumstances, though the atmosphere be normal, too little oxygen is carried to the blood. The minute bronchial tubes are of such a size as to carry a certain quantity of oxygen (in the adult under ordinary circumstances about eighteen cubic feet per day) to the blood. Now if these tubes are contracted it is evident that a smaller quantity of air is inhaled and a smaller quan-

tity of oxygen is absorbed. Now this contraction does sometimes occur. It has been conclusively proved that in asthma the minute bronchial tubes are in a state of spasmodic contraction.—(*Niemeyer's Practice, Vol. 1st, p.* ). The indications of treatment, therefore, in asthma are to relieve the spasm so that the normal quantity of air can enter the lungs, or else to furnish a gas which contains a larger quantity of available oxygen in a given volume than atmospheric air. Both of these indications we think can be fulfilled by chemical means. Carbonic acid when retained in the blood causes relaxation of the muscles, both voluntary and involuntary, anaesthesia, and finally, if oxygen is not furnished in proper quantity, the anaesthesia gives place to asphyxia and death results. It is a well known fact that pressure on the carotid artery, so as to impede the circulation in the brain, causes retention of carbonic acid in the capillaries (where the interchange of gases normally takes place) and anaesthesia is the result. It is plain that carbonic acid gas may be present in the blood in large quantity from the inhalation of this gas; but, bearing in mind the fact that carbonic acid is expelled from the blood owing to the greater affinity of the blood corpuscles for oxygen than for carbonic acid, it is plain that if the oxygen be absorbed, as it were, in some other way, the carbonic acid would remain in the blood and cause relaxation and insensibility. We are not aware that the inhalation of carbonic acid has ever been tried as a remedy for asthma. Dunglison says it has been used much diluted as a sedative, but he does not give any of its special applications. The inhalation of nitrous oxide gas in asthma has recently been strongly advocated by Dr. Holden, of Newark, N. J.— (*American Journal Med. Sciences, Oct.,* 1872). He thinks that its " active principle " is the nitrogen which it contains; but a much more probable explanation of its modus operandi is that it has a great affinity for oxygen, and acts as an absorbent for the oxygen of the air, thus allowing the carbonic acid to remain in the blood and produce its characteristic effects. In this way the bronchial tubes are relaxed, and a sufficient quantity of atmospheric air can enter the air cells. I have no experience with nitrous oxide myself, but my friend Dr. J. W. Scribner, an experienced dentist of Charlottesville, Va., who uses it frequently, tells me that the face and lips become very blue, and that the bleeding is apt to be greater than natural from the extraction of teeth when it is used. Both of these circumstances tend to prove the correctness of the theory advanced above. The second indication in asthma is to furnish a gas which contains a larger quantity of available oxygen in a given volume than atmospheric air under ordinary pressure. The most direct method of fulfilling this indication is to administer pure oxygen gas, and this has frequently been done. Niemeyer speaks favorably of the use of compressed air. The two modes of treatment are obviously incompatible, and as a general rule remedies to relieve the spasm are more used than those which supply oxygen in a concentrated form.

MUCUS.

Mucus is a clear colorless fluid, viscid owing to the presence in it of a peculiar animal principle mucosine. According to Nasse (*Simon loc. cit., p.* 532) the composition of pulmonony mucus is as follows:

| | |
|---|---:|
| Water, | 955.52 |
| Animal Matter, | 33.57 |
| Fat, | 2.89 |
| Chloride of Sodium, | 5.83 |
| Phosphate of Potash and Soda, | 1.05 |
| Sulphate of Potash and Soda, | 0.65 |
| Carbonates of Potash and Soda, | 0.49 |

The composition of mucus doubtless varies somewhat in different parts of the body. Mucosine is not soluble in water, but is soluble in the alkalies and their carbonates. Mucus is sometimes present in too *great* and at other times in too *small* quantity, but so far as is known its secretion is not directly influenced by chemical agents. In old persons, however, and in children or in persons of any age who are much debilitated, the accumulation of mucus in the bronchial tubes may give rise to dangerous symptoms, and may even cause suffocation. Under these circumstances, besides the use of emetics to cause the discharge of the phlegm by vomiting and the relaxation of the muscular fibres of the bronchial tubes, remedies are indicated which have the power of dissolving the mucosine, and thus lessening the consistency of the mucus. Even when persons are not debilitated it is frequently desirable to lessen the consistency of the mucus. Bearing in mind the fact that mucosine is soluble in the alkalies and their carbonates our way is clear, and clinical experience has shown the efficacy of this rational mode of treatment. Inhalation is probably the best mode of administering the remedy when it is desired to lessen the consistency of pulmonary mucus. In some diseases of the stomach, also, as in chronic ulcer and chronic gastric catarrh there is a hyper-secretion of tough mucus and the same treatment by alkalies is indicated. —(*Niemeyer's Practice, Vol. 1st, pp.* 498–499). In treating chronic gastric catarrh, however, the urine should frequently be tested for oxalate of lime, which is very frequently present in the urine in this disease, and if this *is* present the alkaline treatment of the catarrh is contra-indicated. In some forms of diarrhœa and dysentery, also, there is a secretion of thick tenacious mucus, which it is desirable to dissolve. Alkalies are again indicated here on the same grounds. The mucus of the vagina is slightly acid; that of the cervix uteri slightly alkaline.—(*Sim's Ut-rine Surgery, p.* 379). This eminent female surgeon found that the spermatozoa were frequently killed by an excess of acid or of alkali in the female sexual passages. He tested the secretion with litmus, and if it *quickly* turned to a deep pink, he advised alkaline injections; and he mentions two cases in which conception occurred after this treatment when other means had failed. The same distinguished surgeon says (*loc. cit., p.* 385), that there is frequently a muco-purulent discharge from the cervix

4

uteri which kills the spermatozoa. Mr. Swann, of Paris, found that a solution of hydrochloric acid was the only chemical which had the power of dissolving it which did not at the same time kill the spermatozoa. The proportions used by Sims were as follows:

> ℞ Hydrochloric Acid, F. drm. i.
>    Distilled Water, F. dra. vii.
>                      M.

A teaspoonful of this solution in a pint of tepid water was to be thrown in to the vagina night and morning.

CROUP AND DIPTHERIA.—Besides the morbid conditions of mucus, the consideration of croup and diptheria should properly be taken up in this connection, because the fibrinous exudations which are characteristic of these affections usually occur on mucus membranes. In both of these diseases, suffocation is to be apprehended, as the air tubes frequently become blocked up with the exudation. The indication of treatment, therefore, is to dissolve this tough exudation, which consists chiefly of fibrin. We have seen, in a previous section, that the fibrin of the blood is held in solution in that fluid by ammonia, and this agent is highly extolled by Dr. Dagnillon, of Oran, as a remedy for croup and diptheria.—(*Gazette Hebdomadaire, No.* 30. 1870). He applies it directly to the exudation by means of a sponge, and states that in his hands it has proved very beneficial; not only dissolving the exudation already present, but preventing any further formation of the false membrane in the throat. Dr. Steiner, and Dr. Adolph Weber, both recommended lactic acid as a solvent for the exudation, and the former speaks in high terms also of lime water. Lime water was first used by Dr. Steiner, after tracheotomy, to cleanse the tubes, and he injected it up through the opening in the trachea to dissolve the false membranes in the larynx. Finding that no bad consequences resulted from this, he injected it downwards into the larynx before tracheotomy was performed, with the happiest results. Weber administered lactic acid by inhalation, in the dose of fifteen or twenty drops of the acid to half a fluid ounce of water.

Together with this he administered carbonate of soda, by the stomach.

The diptheritic exudation way occur also on the conjunctiva, and give rise to ulceration of the cornea, from the pressure on the vessels, cutting off the supply of nutriment.— (*Stellwag, on the Eye, p.* 301). Under these circumstances, lactic acid or lime water are indicated. The latter should never be used, however, when there is an ulcer of the cornea present. Membranous enteritis (DaCosta) is probably a diptheritic formation, although Dr. H. B. Hare states, that the membrane corresponds most nearly with mucus. It is soluble in caustic alkalies and in sulphuric acid.

## MILK.

A knowledge of the chemical composition of the milk of the human species, and that of the inferior animals, is of very great importance to every physician who treats the diseases of infants and children. The composition of human milk, and that of the cow, the ass, the goat, and the ewe, is given in the table below, which is taken from West, on diseases of children, p. 443:

| | SP. GRAVITY. | FLUID. | SOLIDS. | SUGAR. | BUTTER. | CASEINE AND EXTRACTIVE. | INCOMBUSTIBLE SALTS. |
|---|---|---|---|---|---|---|---|
| Man......................... | 1,032.67 | 889.08 | 110.92 | 43.64 | 26.66 | 39.24 | 1.38 |
| Cow......................... | 1,033.38 | 864.06 | 135.94 | 38.03 | 36.12 | 55.15 | 6.61 |
| Ass......................... | 1,634.57 | 890.12 | 109.88 | 50.46 | 18.53 | 36.65 | 5.21 |
| Goat........................ | 1,033.53 | 844.90 | 155.10 | 36.91 | 56.87 | 55.14 | 6.18 |
| Ewe......................... | 1,040.98 | 832.32 | 167.68 | 39.43 | 54.31 | 69.78 | 7.16 |

The milk of all animals, varies of course, at different times, but the table given above shows the average composition. When the secretion of milk in the human female is scanty, electricity is sometimes of service in increasing it. When it becomes necessary to raise a child by hand, that diet should be selected which most nearly corresponds with its natural food. Cow's milk, from the facility with which it is obtained, is most generally substituted for the mother's milk, but as a general rule it is mixed with an equal quantity of water, or a mixture is made of one-third milk and two-thirds water. In nearly all books on the subject of childrens' diseases we find the very great dilution of milk advised. It is evident, on a moments reflection, that this is an extremely irrational mode of preparing a substitute for the natural food of the infant. The child has to take a much larger quantity into the stomach to get a proper supply of nourishment, and this overloading of the infant's stomach is the starting point to numberless ailments. It will be seen by reference to the table, that cow's milk has more of all the solid constituents, except sugar, and the aggregate amount of the solids in cow's milk is rather greater than in human milk. Cow's milk containing about two and a-half per cent. more solids than that of the human female. Besides this quantitative difference, there is a qualitative difference between human milk and that of the cow. This difference consists in the casein of human milk coagulating in small floculi, while that of cow's milk coagulates in large lumps. This coagulation in lumps prevents its proper solution by the gastric juice ; and it passes out of the stomach to act as an iritant to the mucous membrane of the bowels. To prevent this coagulation in lumps, Meigs and Pepper, and also Dr. Eustace Smith, advise the administration of gelatin, to act mechanically by separating the particles of caseine and causing it to coagulate in smaller particles. The best artificial food for infants then seems to be cow's milk with a small quantity of water, or what is better, because it is a solvent for caseine, lime water added to it and a little gelatin.

TEARS.

The tears consist of water, 99.06.    Solids, 00.94.    No chemical changes occur in it as far as we know.

SEBACEOUS MATTER.

The sebaceous matter is an oeaginous fluid, having, according to Esenbeck, (*Wilson on diseases of the Skin, London edition, p.* 50.) the following composition :

| | | | | | | |
|---|---|---|---|---|---|---|
| Fat, | - | - | - | - | - | 24.2 |
| Osmazone, with traces of oil, | | - | | - | - | 12.6 |
| Watery Extractive, | - | - | - | - | | 11.6 |
| Albumen and Caseine, | | - | - | - | - | 24.2 |
| Carbonate of Lime, | - | - | - | - | | 2.1 |
| Phosphate of Lime, . | | - | - | - | - | 20.0 |
| Carbonate of Magnesia, | - | - | - | - | | 1.6 |
| Acetate and Muriate of Soda and loss, | | | - | | - | 3.7 |

100.0

The secretion of sebaceous matter is sometimes excessive and sometimes diminished in quantity. When excessive, the use of alkaline washes has been recommended by Wilson, with the view of forming a soap by the union of the alkali with the oil and fat of the sebaceous matter. When diminished in quantity, it is necessary to furnish some substitute in order to lubricate the skin and keep it soft. Glycerine is very generally used for this purpose. Changes doubtless occur in the quality of the sebaceous matter, but with our present knowledge but little can be said on this point. Wilson describes a qualitative change in this secretion which he called stearrhoea nigricans. Dr. Owen Rees examined the secretion and found it to consist of carbon, iron, lime, albuminous matters, fatty matter, and chloride and phosphate of soda.

### SALIVA.

The saliva is secreted chiefly by the parotid, sub-maxillary and sub-lingual glands. Its composition according to Bidder and Schmidt, Flint's Physiology, vol. 2d, p. 171, is as follows :

| | | | | | | |
|---|---|---|---|---|---|---|
| Water, | - | - | - | - | - | 995.16 |
| Epithelium, | - | - | - | - | - | 1.62 |
| Soluble Organic Matter, | - | - | - | - | | 1.34 |
| Sulpho-cyanide of Potassium, | | | - | | . | 0.06 |
| Phosphate of Soda, Lime, and Magnesia, | | | | - | | 0.98 |
| Chloride of Potassium and Sodium, | - | | - | | - | 0.84 |

1,000.00

The function of saliva in the human species is not definitely known. Some physiologists say it has only a mechanical function, while others contend that it is one of the means by which starch is converted into sugar. It certainly has the power of causing this conversion, but it is generally believed that the gastric juice is the chief agent in this transformation. Nothing is known concerning the composition of saliva in diseases which is of any clinical significance.

GASTRIC JUICE.

The gastric juice is the fluid secreted by the gastric follicles of the stomach, and it is intended for the digestion of nitrogenized articles of food. Its composition according to Dalton, is as follows :

| | |
|---|---:|
| Water, - - - - - - | 975.80 |
| Organic Matter, - - - - | 15.70 |
| Lactic Acid, - - - - - | 4.00 |
| Chloride of Sodium, - - - | 1.70 |
| Chloride of Potassium, - - - | 1.08 |
| Chloride of Calcium, - - - | 0.20 |
| Chloride of Ammonium, - - - | 0.65 |
| Phosphate of Lime, - - - | 1.48 |
| Phosphate of Magnesia, - - - | 0.04 |
| Phosphate of Iron, - - - | 0.05 |
| | 1,000.00 |

Many physiological chemists have found hydro-chloric instead of lactic acid in the gastric juice. Others have thought the acidity was owing to the acid phosphate of lime. The general opinion at the present day is in favor of lactic acid. *All* agree in the presence of some acid and it is a fact well known to every practitioner of medicine that it is sometimes present in excess. Whether it is a hypersecretion of the acid principle alone, or whether the gastric juice itself is secreted in abnormal quantity, is not determined. The former is probably the correct explanation. There may be an excess of acid in the stomach from other causes, as when a child takes food into its stomach which it is unable to digest properly, and which by decomposition forms an excess of acid. This acid dyspepsia of children has been very ably described by Dr

Eustace Smith in the American Journal of Obstetrics, &c., for 1872. In other cases the quantity and quality of the gastric juice may be normal, but owing to an inflamed and irritated state of the mucous membrane of the stomach, the normal juice becomes too irritating. This is probably the state of affairs in pregnancy, and the beneficial action of magnesia and other antacids is doubtless owing to their power of counteracting the acid principle of the gastric juice, and thus rendering it less irritating. In all cases when the acid is in excess, or when the normal amount is too irritating, *antacids* are indicated. The carbonates of the alkalies are probably most generally employed.—(*Niemeyer*). Lime water is very popular with many physicians, especially when combined with sub-nitrate of bismuth. Headland states that the action of bismuth is purely mechanical, but the experience of the great majority of physicians is in favor of its being an *antacid*. Effervescing mixtures containing a tartrate or citrate of potash or soda have been advised, and lemonade is highly extolled by some physicians. The *citrate* of potash of the lemon juice is converted into the *carbonate*, which in its turn is decomposed, the potash uniting with the acid of the stomach and the carbonic acid being discharged by eructation.

The organic principle of the gastric juice, "pepsin," is peculiar to that fluid, and is necessary for digestion. This substance may sometimes be in excess in the gastric juice, but nothing is known of such a condition if it ever occurs. It is frequently, however, diminished in quantity, and this diminution may be either temporary or permanent. Drs. Fenwick and Flint, Sr., have proved quite conclusively that the pathology of Addison's disease is atrophy of the gastric tubules. In this disease the secretion of gastric juice is, of course, diminished in proportion to the number of tubules affected. Life could *possibly* be prolonged in these cases by the administration of an artificial gastric juice. So far as I know, however, nothing of the kind has ever been tried. When the diminution in the secretion is only temporary, as after attacks

of severe illness, the administration of pepsin has been tried
with decided benefit ; and if the "great expectations" concerning the benefit to be derived from pepsin have not been
fully realized, it is probably owing, in part, to the fact, that
much of the pepsin now in use is obtained from the stomach of the cow an herbivorous animal, and is given to take
the place of that of man an omnivorous animal.

### PANCREATIC JUICE.

The pancreatic juice is secreted by the pancreas. Nothing is known concerning the chemical composition of this
fluid in the human subject. That obtained from the dog has
been analysed and the composition of that of man has been
inferred from this. It is scarcely necessary to give the composition of this fluid taken from the dog. It contains a much
larger proportion of organic matter than any of the other
fluids, and this matter is called *pancreatine*, and is the principle agent in the digestion of fat which is converted into an
emulsion by it. This substance is undoubtedly present in
human as well as in canine pancreatic juice, and its function
is the same in all animals. Nothing definite is known concerning the abnormal condition of this fluid. It is highly
probable, however, that some cases of "fatty diarrhœa" are
owing to a deficient secretion of pancreatic juice, and pancre-
antic has been already used in such cases with decided benefit.

### INTESTINAL JUICE.

Concerning the intestinal juice even less is known than
about pancreatic juice. Its reaction in the dog is alkaline and
its function seems to be to assist in the conversion of starch
into sugar. Nothing is known concerning its chemical composition in man, and, of course, nothing can be known concerning its abnormal conditions.

### BILE.

The bile is secreted by the liver. Its most important constituents are glyco-cholate and tauro-cholate of soda. Its
function is not definitely known, but it is certainly, in some

way, connected with the process of digestion, for when the secretion of bile is checked from any cause, or its entrance into the intestine prevented, imperfect and painful digestion is the result.

Medicines to promote the secretion of bile have been used from time immemorial, but not with any very definite views as to their *modus operandi*. Headland (*loc: cit.*), states that *quinine* has been found of great benefit in acholia, and he thinks it acts by taking the place of the taurine of bile, to which it is precisely similar in its chemical composition. As taurine can now be manufactured synthetically from sulphuric acid, alchohol, and ammonia (*Odling*), at a very low price, it would be advisable, if Mr. Headland's theory be correct, to use this artificial taurine in these cases in the place of quinine. If the acholia were prolonged, however, substances to take the place of taurine would do but little good, as the retention of cholesterine would cause the most prominent and most dangerous symptoms. The presence of the bile pigments, &c., in other secretions and excretions will be treated of while speaking of the fluids in which they are found.

Choleate of soda has recently been proposed as a remedy for biliary lithiasis, by Prof. Schiff, on the ground that as bile stones usually consist chiefly of cholesterine, and as this substance is soluble in choleate of soda, the bile stones can thus be dissolved, and their formation prevented. He says the treatment has been tried, and found of very decided benefit. He administers the remedy in the dose of about seven and a half grains twice a day, gradually increasing till the system becomes saturated.

### SERUM.

The secretion of serous membranes is known as serum. Its function is to keep the membrane soft and pliable. The composition of serum is not definitely known, but it contains albumen in large quantity and some chloride of sodium. A knowledge of its proximate composition has been utilized by

5

Dr. Peaslee in the operation of ovariotomy. He advises that during the operation the hands of the operator be frequently bathed in an artificial serum having the following composition:

R  Chloride of Sodium, dra. iv.
   White of Egg, dra. vi.
   Water, P. iv.
                              M.

So far as we can learn this is the only practical use which has been made of a knowledge of the composition of the secretion of serous membranes.

———

The fluids of the organism, which are excerctions, are perspiration, urine, and bile. The latter, as we have before stated, has a double office, to assist in digestion and to carry off the cholesterine excreted by the liver. Cholesteraemia has been already treated of under the head of the Blood, and we shall not refer to it again.

### PERSPIRATION.

The perspiration is a colorless, watery fluid, having a distinctly acid reaction. Its composition, according to Anselmino, (*Simon loc. cit., p.* 374) is as follows:

Water,            -      -      -      -      -      - 995.000
Epidermis and Salts of Lime,   -      -      -      .100
Water Extract and Sulphates,   -      -      - 1.050
Spirit Extract, Chlorides of Sodium and Potash,  2.400
Alcohol Extract, Acetates Lactates and Free Lactic
   Acid,      -      -      -      -      - 1.450

The gases given off by the skin are, according to Collard de Martigny, carbonic acid and nitrogen. The chief function of the perspiration is to regulate the temperature of the body. When exposed to a high temperature the secretion of perspiration is very copious, and in its evaporation and passage to the gaseous form, so much heat becomes latent that the temperature of the body is reduced to the normal standard. Besides this function, however, the perspiration has another important function, namely, the elimination of effete matters from the system. As we have seen in a previous section, the skin is one of the channels for the vicarious elimination of urea when its elimination by the kidneys is interfered with. So in rheumatism, the lactic acid is eliminated by the skin, and has been found in the perspiration in considerable quantity. Uric acid and urate of soda have also been found in the perspiration, and it is highly probable that these substances are eliminated by the skin to a certain extent in gout. Albumen has been found in the sweat by Anselmino and Stark, but the circumstances under which it is present are not sufficiently known to lead to any practical results. The coloring matter of the bile is present in the perspiration whenever from any cause its secretion or its passage into the intestines is interfered with. In all those diseases where the " materies morbi" is eliminated by the skin remedies are indicated which increase the discharge of perspiration. None of the diaphoretics have a directly chemical action. Water should be drunk in considerable quantity so as to take the place of that which passes off as perspiration. The discharge of carbonic acid by the skin is not very great, and so far as we are aware only one physiologist has drawn any practical deduction from it. Claude Bernard advances the theory that the greater rate of mortality after amputations in the upper part of a limb than in the lower is owing to a larger surface for the excretion of carbonic acid being removed in the former than in the latter. This is simply a theory, and requires further examination before any definite conclusions can be reached.

## URINE.

The urine is an excretion, and it is in this fluid that the effete nitrogenized matters are discharged from the system. The chemical composition of the urine in health has long been known.

According to the analysis of Berzelius, Lehman and Becquerel it is as follows :

Water,  -  -  -  -  -  - 938.00
Urea,  -  -  -  -  -  - 30.00
Creatine,  -  -  -  -  - 1.25
Creatinine,  -  -  -  -  - 1.50
Urates of Soda, Potassa and Ammonia,  -  - 180
Coloring Matter and Mucus,  -  -  - .30
Bi-Phosphate of Soda, ⎫
Phosphate of Soda,   |
    "   * of Potassa, ⎬  -  -  - 12.45
    "    of Magnesia, |
    "    of Lime, ⎭
Chlorides of Sodium and Potassium,  -  - 7.80
Sulphate of Soda and Potassa,  -  -  - 6.90

Healthy urine has generally an acid reaction, but as shown by Dr. Bence Jones and others it is frequently alkaline soon after eating. The specific gravity is about 1020. A knowledge of the changes which take place in the urine after its discharge from the body, and the order in which these changes occur, is absolutly necessary before we can understand the abnormal conditions of this fluid ; hence we shall consider these changes briefly.

After standing a few hours the *epithelium* and mucus are deposited in the form of a light flocculent precipitate. The next change which takes place is the acid fermentation. This is caused by the formation of lactic acid in some way as yet not understood. (By reference to the table we see that there is no free acid in the urine, the acid reaction being caused by the bi-phosphate of soda). The lactic acid decomposes a portion of the urates and uric acid is deposited. Oxalic acid is also frequently formed during the acid fermentation, and this uniting with the lime causes a deposit of crystals of oxalate of lime. After some days the alkaline fermentation begins when the urea is converted into carbonate of ammonia and the earthy phosphates are deposited, and by double decomposition the triple phosphate of magnesia and ammonia, and the phosphate of soda and ammonia are formed. These salts form crystals which can be seen in all parts of the fluid.

Having thus taken a short view of the composition of the urine in health, and the changes which it undergoes after being discharged from the body, we are prepared to study its abnormal conditions and their clinical significance. We shall consider first those abnormal substances which are in solution in the urine and subsequently take up "urinary deposits." The substances in solution in the urine which are symptomatic of disease of some organ of the body are: Albumen, sugar, biliary matter, fat, leucine and tyrosine.

1. ALBUMINURIA.—Albuminous urine according to Niemeyer (*Practice of Medicine, Vol.* 2, *p.* 26,) is generally of a pale yellow color, and often exhibits somewhat of an opalescent reflection. As it is more viscid than common urine, on account of the albumen which it contains, it is more easily made frothy than urine free from albumen, and the froth lasts longer. When there is no intercurrent febrile disease the specific gravity is remarkably low, and may sink to 1,005. The physical characteristics of albuminous urine are very variable, but the chemical tests are very simple. When heated to 167° Fhr. albumen coagulates if the fluid which contains it be neutral or slightly acid. It is also coagulated by the mineral acids. Nitric acid is generally used for this purpose. If, however, a very small quantity of nitric acid be added to urine containing albumen, and it is then heated, the albumen is not precipitated.—(*Odling, p.* 194). In order to avoid any mistake the suspected urine should be tested in both ways. Albuminuria is generally a symptom of Bright's disease of the kidneys, but it may be caused by any form of congestion of the kidney. It sometimes occurs during pregnancy, and is then a sign that uraemic poisoning is threatened. We have already stated that when albumen is present in the urine, there is an excess of urea in the blood. The connection between albuminous urine and puerperal convulsions is thus explained, and the importance of examining the urine during

pregnancy for albumen is ably pointed out by the late Dr. Geo. T. Elliot in his "Obstetric Clinic." There is probably no causative relation existing between the presence of albumen in the urine and the retention of urea in the blood. Both are doubtless owing to the congestion of the kidneys, and the loss of the epithelial lining of the uriniferous tubules.—(*Niemeyer*).

The indications of treatment to which the presence of albumen in the urine give rise have already been treated of under the head of "Uraemia." A few rymarks concerning the diet suitable in albuminuria, however, are called for in this connection. We have seen previously that when albuminuria exists, the amount of albumen in the blood is below the normal standard, and that under these circumstances dropsy is liable to occur. We should therefore give food rich in albumen, to take the place of that drained off by the kidneys. Eggs contain albumen in larger quantity than any other alimentary substance, and owing to the large quantity of inorganic alimentary·principles which they contain, are peculiarly suitable as an article of diet. Milk is also very suitable as the casein which it contains is converted into albumen before being absorbed. Both eggs and milk are very easy of digestion. If the patient is sufficiently strong to digest it, meat should be used, as the musculine of meat, like the casein of milk, is converted into albumen before being absorbed.

Vegetable albumen is found most abundantly in turnips, carrots, cabbages, &c.—(*Flint's Physiologo, Vol.* 1, *p.* 51).

2. DIABETES MELLITUS.—Urine, which contains sugar, can not be distinguished by the eye from the normal secretion. Its specific gravity is, on an average, 1,035. It has a distinctly sweetish taste, and like albuminous urine retains its froth for some time after being agitated.

But little of a definite nature is known concerning the function of sugar in the animal economy. The general opinion among physiologists is that it is in some way connected with the production of animal heat.

In certain conditions of the system sugar may appear in

the urine temporarily and in small quantity, without being a symptom of any serious disease. When it continues for a length of time, however, and is present in large quantity, it is a symptom of great gravity. The cause of its appearance in the urine is unknown ; that there is an increased production in the liver is certain, (*Flint's Physiology, Vol.* 1, *p.* 59); and it is probable that in some cases, at least, less sugar is consumed in the animal economy than in a state of health.

It is a matter of great importance, on account of the prognosis, to be able to detect sugar in the urine, and various tests have been proposed for this purpose. The one in most general use is Trommer's, which is practiced in the following manner: To the suspected fluid add a few drops of liquor potassæ, to render it distinctly alkaline ; then add a small quantity of a moderately strong solution of sulphate of copper, and heat the fluid in a test tube ; if sugar be present, a little before the boiling point is reached a red precipitate of suboxide of copper is formed. In Böttger's test subnitrate of bismuth is used instead of sulphate of copper, and carbonate of soda instead of liquor potassea. A black precipitate is formed in this test. There are several other tests, but they possess no advantages over those given above.

As so little is known concerning the physiology and pathology of the formation of sugar, but little of a definite nature can be said concerning the treatment of diabetes mellitus on chemical principles. Under the supposition that sugar was converted into lactic acid in the lungs, and then united with alkalies to form salts, alkaline remedies were proposed, and it is thought by some that their use was attended with benefit.—(*Flint's practice, p.* 81). Acids to prevent the transformation of amylum into sugar have been proposed, as has also yeast, to act as a ferment, and cause the sugar produced in the liver to be converted into lactic acid. None of these proposed remedies have come up to expectations, although they have sometimes seemed to be of service. Cantani recommended lactic acid. He thought diabetes was owing to the formation of a substance called paraglucose, which could not be burnt off, and consequently the fat and albumen were burnt off to keep up the animal heat. Lactic acid has been extensively used and highly extolled by most physicians who have used it.—*See an article in Edinburgh Med. Journal for December,* 1871, *by Dr. G. W. Balfour*). Skim milk, proposed by Dr. Arthur Scott Donkin, would act by virtue of the lactic acid which it contains.

The diet is agreed on all hands to be of the utmost importance. All saccharine and amylaceous articles should be avoided. Meat, eggs, fish, &c., are useful. A small quantity of bread daily is very necessary to the comfort of the patient, and does no serious harm. The following list of vegetables, arranged in order according to their proportion of starch, is given on the authority of Payen, in Flint's physiology, Vol. 2d, p. 37: Parsnips, which contain in their natural condition 6, and dessicated 29.38 parts per 100 of starch ; carrots, pods of string beans, turnips. Starch is found principally in the cortical portion of these roots. Cabbage ; the presence of starch is recognized in very small quantity in the ribs of the leaves. Cauliflower ; in the upper extremity or head are slight traces, No starch was found in romain, lettuce, chiccory, in the leaves of sorrel, spinage, asparagus, artichauts, leeks, nor in the large early white onion. Sugar is found as such in some of the articles in the foregoing list in considerable quantity. Onions and turnips both contain sugar in some quantity, and parsnips and carrots contain both sugar and starch.

3. Biliary matter is present in the urine in jaundice from whatever cause the disease may have arisen. It is occasionally of importance, in a diagnostic point of view, to determine the presence or absence of the coloring matter of the bile. It is doubtful whether the urine as voided ever contains more than a trace of the true biliary salts.—(*Odling*). The two most common tests for the biliary coloring matter in the urine are known respectively as the nitric acid test and Heller's test.

"In the nitric acid test a little of the urine, previously concentrated if necessary, is poured on a white slab and a few
drops of nitric acid then let fall upon it. Where the acid comes
in contact with the biliary urine there is a peculiar play of
colors produced—green, pink, violet and yellow being easily
recognizable."—(*Odling*).

In Heller's test it is necessary that albumen be present in
the urine, and hence white of egg has to be added. On the
addition of nitric acid a cloud is formed of a somewhat bluish
color. When a sample of urine containing biliary matter
is exhibited, a yellow scum is formed on the surface.—
*Galloway's Qualitative Chemical Analysis, p.* 315).

4. Frerichs found that in "Acute yellow atrophy of the
liver," leucine and tyrosine were always present in the urine
in large quantity.—(*Niemeyer*). Leucine has been found by
different chemists, in nearly every tissue of the body, but the
only one which contains it in health, so far as we know at
present, is the spleen. According to Hoppe-Seyler, it is
generally produced by the splitting up of albuminoid substances. The observations of this chemist, and of others,
render it highly probable that further chemical examination
of the faeces for this substance, and also for tyrosine, will
throw much light on a class of affections (diseases of the pancreas), the nature of which is now very imperfectly understood.
In an able article in the American Journal of the Medical
Sciences, for January, 1872, by Dr. James Tyson, of Philadelphia, we find the following tests for leucine: It crystalizes
in spherules which are generally colored yellow by the coloring
matter of the bile. If a portion of the deposit from the urine
be heated in a dry test-tube, over a lamp, and leucine is present, it will be converted by boiling into an oily drop, and
emit an odor like burnt horn. Another test is: if leucine be
heated in an open tube to the temperature of 170° Fhr. it
sublimes and gives off flocculent wooly masses. This test is
very characteristic.

5. The same remarks which were made relative to leucine

will apply to *tyrosine.* The pathological conditions under which they most frequently appear in the urine are in atrophic conditions of the liver. There are several tests for tyrosine given by Dr. Tyson in the paper referred to above, but we shall only give one or two of them here. Hoffman's test is practiced in the following manner: Dissolve a small quantity of the suspected crystals in a test-tube; add a few drops of a solution of nitrate of mercury and heat to boiling. If tyrosine is present the liquid will soon change to a rosy red, and later a red precipitate takes place. On the application of heat to tyrosine it gives off the odor of burnt horn, but does not sublime as does leucine. Urine which contains these substances is generally deficient in urea, and death seems generally caused by uraemic poisoning. Their presence generally indicates a speedy course for the disease in connection with which they appear

Medicines to promote the vicarious elimination of urea are generally indicated. With this exception there seems to be no special therapeutical indications. The diseases in which they appear in the urine are nearly always fatal.

6. Fat is occasionally present in the urine. It is easily detected by the microscope. It appears as round shining globules with dark edges. The presence of kiestein, a fatty substance, in the urine was formerly considered characteristic of pregnancy, but this has been disproved. It is of no clinical significance.—(*See Elliot's Obstetric Clinic*).

———

Urinary Deposits—Urinary deposits may be either inorganic or organic compounds. The most common forms of deposit are urate of ammonia, earthy phosphates, oxalate of lime, and uric acid. These may be present either singly or combined with each other. The following table is given by Bowman, (*Medical Chemistry, p.* 3) for facilitating the examination of urinary deposits by means of chemical tests:

(1) The sediment dissolves when warmed; *Urate of Am-*

*monia.* Not soluble when warmed; but, (2) soluble in acetic acid; *Earthy Phosphates.* Insoluble in acetic acid; but, (3) soluble in dilute hydrochloric acid; *Oxalate of Lime.* Insoluble in dilute hydrocloric acid; but, (4) purple with nitric acid and ammonia; *Uric Acid.*

If the deposit proves to be none of the above, it must be one of the following:

(5) Greenish yellow deposit easily diffused on agitation; *Pus.* (6) Ropy and tenacious; *Mucus?* (7) Red or brown; not soluble when warmed; the fluid portion coagulable by heat and nitric acid; *Blood.* (8) Soluble in ammonia; the solution leaving on evaporation hexagonal crystals; *Cystine.* (9) Yellowish sediment; soluble when warmed; *Urate of Soda?* (10) Ether yields after agitation an oily or fatty residue; *Fatty Matter.* (11) Milky appearance; *Chylous Matter.*

Bowman also gives at pp. 119–120 a table for facilitating the microscopical examination of urinary deposits which are given below.

1. If the deposit is crystaline:

(1) Lozenge shaped crystals; *Uric Acid.* (2) Stellae, or three sided prisms; *Triple Phosphate.* (3) Octahedra, or dumb-bells; *Oxalate of Lime.* (4) Rosette-like tables; *Cystine.*

2. If amorphous or rounded particles:

(1) Soluble when warmed; *Urate of Ammonia.* (2) Soluble in acetic acid; *Phosphate of Lime.* (3) Yellowish grains; *Urate of Soda.* (4) Round globules with dark edges; *Fatty Matter.* (5) White and milky; *Chylous Matter.*

3. If organized particles:

(1) Granulated corpuscles in stringy aggregation; *Mucus.* (2) Irregularly shaped scales; *Epithelium.* (3) Detached granulated corpuscles; *Pus.* (4) Blood corpuscles; *Blood.* (5) Spermatozoa; *Semen.*

A table for facilitating the examination of urinary deposits is given by Galloway (*loc : cit, pp.* 317–320), but it is neither so complete nor so simple as the table given above, and we think it entirely unnecessary to reproduce it here.

We shall now proceed to study each of these deposits in the order in which they are given in the "table for facilitating the examination of urinary deposits by means of chemical tests."

URIC ACID DIATHESIS.—Urate of ammonia generally occurs in acid urine. It is important because one form of calculus is composed of it. This form of calculus is combustible; soluble in nitric acid yielding uric acid reaction; soluble also in boiling water and carbonates of alkalies. Bearing this fact in mind, alkalies and their carbonates would seem to be indicated. The Vichy water which contains carbonates of lime, soda and magnesia, sulphate of soda, chloride of sodium, and some free carbonic acid, is highly recommended by Erichsen. He also speaks favorably of the use of bicarbonate of potash and nitre. The carbonate of lithia and lithia water have been much used of late years.—(*See section on Gout*). When administering alkalies in the uric acid diathesis, the urine should be frequently tested to see whether it is acid or alkaline, else the uric acid, diathesis, may give place to the phosphatic. Calculi consisting of alternate layers of different chemical compounds are by no means rare. Acid fruits are contra-indicated in the uric acid diathesis as a general thing, except those acids, such as lemon juice, which contain a large amount of potash. The malates, tartrates, citrates, &c., are converted into carbonates in the stomach, and enter the blood as such. Bird says (*Urinary Deposits, p.* 132), that roasted apples, strawberries, currants, and some other fruits may occasionally be employed with advantage, and I have, on one occasion, seen great benefit result from the use of grapes.

OXALIC DIATHESIS.—The oxalic diathesis according to Golding Bird is one of the most common. It occurs in urine in which there is an abnormally large quantity of urea, and Bird thinks the oxalic acid is formed sometimes from urea, by the oxidation of this substance. Oxalate of lime calculi are quite common. They generally, however, have a nucleus of uric acid or urate of soda. They are incombustible and infusible ; and are soluble slowly in nitric and hydrochloric acids without effervescence. Oxalate of lime in persons in good health does not enter the blood, or reach the urine, on account of its insolubility. Certain vegetables, such as the rhubarb plant, sorrel, tomatoes and turnips, contain enough of a soluble salt of oxalic acid to cause a deposit of oxalate of lime in the urine. Onions, although containing a salt of oxalic acid, do not cause oxaluria, because the oxalate which they contain is insoluble.

The treatment should be directed to causing the solution of the deposit of oxalate of lime. For this purpose nitric and hydrochloric acid, or a mixture of the two, should be given, and their use kept up some time.

The vegetables previously mentioned containing a large quantity of oxalic acid, and also those containing sugar in large quantity, should be avoided.—(*Gross' System of Surgery*, *Vol.* 2, *p.* 760).

PHOSPHATIC DIATHESIS.—The phosphatic deposit may occur in three forms : (1) Triple or ammonio-magnesian phosphate. (2) Phosphate of lime , and (3), a mixture of the above.

The urine in this diathesis is either neutral or feebly acid in reaction. It frequently becomes alkaline, however, soon after being passed. The phosphatic are the most common forms of calculi. They are soluble in dilute hydrochloric and nitric acid, and the triple phosphate is also soluble in acetic acid. The mineral acids, especially nitric, are recommended in this diathesis.

Attention to the general health is of the utmost importance in all these affections, but as chemistry has nothing to do with the general treatment, it does not claim our attention.

PYURIA.—Pus is usually found·in acid or neutral urine. It is symptomatic of suppurative disease of the kidneys or urinary passages. When it occurs it is in the form of a greenish layer at the bottom of the vessel, and can easily be diffused through the urine. If the urine be alkaline, however, or if an alkali be added to it, the pus becomes coagulated, and either hangs in shreds or forms a coagulum of greater or less firmness. The microscopic characters have been previously given. The therapeutical indications will of course depend upon the nature of the disease under wich the patient labors, and hence no general rule gan be given in this connection with regard to treatment.

URINE CONTAINING MUCUS.—Mucus is generally present in the urine in very small quantity. When present in large quantity it is generally symptomatic of inflammation of the bladder, either sub-acute or chronic. It differs from pus in being in shreds and strings even when the urine is acid. When acetic acid is added to urine containing mucus, the fluid portion of the mucus coagulates into a thin corrugated membrane. (*Bird*). The presence of mucus gives rise to no special indications of treatment.

HAEMATURIA.—Blood may be present in the urine either from disease or injury of the kidneys or urinary passages. It is generally easily detected by the microscope, and by the spontaneous coagulation of the fibrin. Chemistry bears no part in its treatment that we need consider in this connection. The *modus operandi* of astringents will be briefly considered elsewhere.

CYSTINE IN THE URINE.—Cystine is not a common form of urinary deposit, but is of interest from the fact that occasionally calculi occur, which are composed of it. It generally appears as a white or pale fawn-colored powder. It is soluble in the mineral, but insoluble in the vegetable acids. Is also freely soluble in ammonia and the fixed alkalies and their carbonates, but is insoluble in carbonate of ammonia. On being kept for a short time, cystic urine becomes covered with a greasy looking pellicle. The presence of this substance in the urine seems to be hereditary and generally intimately connected with scrofula. Too little is known on the subject for any definite rules to be laid down concerning the treatment ; bearing in mind, however, its ready solubility in the mineral acids and also in ammonia and the alkalies, these would seem to be indicated ; the acids when the urine was alkaline, and *vice versa.* Epithelium and urinary casts are occasionally present in the urine, and may be detected by the microscope. They do dot demand our attention in this connection, however.

## PART II.

Having now completed the consideration of the fluids of the organism, we will proceed to study the solids. Only those will be considered, however, a knowledge of whose chemical composition is of service to the medical practitioner. Faeces, although semi-solid, will be considered under this head.

We propose, then, to study the solids of the organism in the following order :

(1) Nervous tissue. (2) Muscular tissue. (3) Bony tissue. (4) Hair. (5) Coats of arteries. (6) Faeces.

### NERVOUS TISSUE.

The chemical composition of nervous matter is a subject to which very little importance has been attached, but it is one which we are convinced is well worth investigation. We learn from Turner's Chemistry that nervous matter consists of 80 per cent. of water, 7 per cent. of albumen, and that the remainder is fatty matter. It is to this fatty matter that we will direct our attention.

The fatty matter is in the form of two acids, *cerebric* and *oleo-phosphoric.*

Cerebric is distinguished from the other fatty acids by containing nitrogen and phosphorus. The other acid, oleo phosphoric, as its name implies, is composed of phosphorus and fat. The precise function of these acids is unknown. Many chemists have found an excess of the earthy phosphates in the urine after severe and prolonged mental exertion. It is true that this view, of the discharge of phosphorus by the kidneys has been opposed (*See American Journal Medical Sciences, April,* 1870, *pp.* 506–507); but we think the grounds of opposition are insufficient. It has been found, too, that if phosphorus be supplied in some form, it acts as food for the overtasked brain and refreshes the weary mind. Dr. Judson B. Andrews, of the New York State Lunatic Asylum, in the American Journal of Insanity for October, 1869, gives the result of his experience with phosphoric acid. It acts, he says, as a special nervous stimulant. Dr. Wm. A. Hammond, arguing from the chemical composition of the brain, and from the fact that phosphorus is discharged in large quantity by the kidneys, after severe mental effort, has proposed phosphorated oil in the treatment of mental depression and wakefulness brought on by over-exertion of the mind, and its use has been attended with great benefit in nearly every case. This form of disease is confined chiefly to professional men, and doubtless sweeps many of our ablest thinkers to the grave. It is probably to this cause that Horace Greeley owed his death.

Let us bear in mind also that nervous matter contains a large proportion of fat. This fact suggests valuable therapeutical indications. That neuralgia is frequently owing to a want of some of the normal constituents of the nervous matter cannot be doubted, and Dr. F. E. Anstie, in "Diseases of the Spine and of the Nerves," says he has found fat of very great benefit in the treatment of this disease. He usually gives cod-liver oil, but if this can not be borne he gives cream. The writer of this article has been, from a child, subject to violent attacks of frontal neuralgia, and he has found that when he habitually takes a large amount of butter with his food the attacks are less frequent and less severe.

### MUSCULAR TISSUE.

Muscular tissue contains about 17 per cent. of fibrin, cells, vessels, and nerves, and about 2.30 per cent. of albumen. It is unnecessary to give the composition of muscular tissue in full, as we shall only have occasion to speak of the fibrinous and albuminous principles. We propose to consider these principles briefly in connection with the *modus operandi* of astringents. Mialhe, (*Chemie applique a la physiologie et a la therapeutique, p.* 646) says *:* "Vous les astringents apparticnnent à la classe des coagulants ; cést-a-dire à la classe des agents chemiques, susceptibles d'entrer en combinaison avec les elements albumineux du sang et de former avec eux un composé in-soluble." Headland says that not only have astringents the power of coagulating albumen, but also of causing the coagulation of fibrine, and he thinks that it is by this coagulation and consequent hardening that astringents act. The *modus operandi* of ergotine is not very definite ; it certainly has the power of lessening the calibre of bloodvessels, and its action as a parturifacient is universally acknowledged, but it is impossible, for obvious reasons, that the very great contraction of the uterus, which frequently occurs under its use, should be owing entirely to the coagulation of the fibrin and albumen contained in muscular tissue. Mialhe confesses his inability to account for its action on chemical principles.

### BONE.

The chemical composition of bone and the alterations which take place in it in disease, have been very carefully and thoroughly studied. The constituents of bone to which we have to direct our attention are only two—the phosphate and the carbonate of lime. The former is by far the most important inorganic principle of bone. Lassaigne found that it was present in healthy bone in the proportion of 400 parts per 1,000. It is intimately associated with the organic matter of bone, and can only be separated from it by chemical means. When allowed to stand in hydrochloric acid the bone becomes flexible in consequence of the phosphate of lime being decomposed and withdrawn from combination with the organic matter. Bostock found that phosphate of lime was present in the vertebra of a rachitic patient in the proportion of 136 parts per 1,000. The practical importance of a knowledge of this fact is apparent at a glance. The indication is to supply phosphate

7

of lime. The administration of pure phosphate of lime has not been attended with as much benefit as was expected from it. The *lacto*-phosphate is said to answer admirably as a remedy in this affection.—(*Parry, in American Journal Medical Sciences, April*, 1872).

### HAIR.

Hair contains nearly 5 per cent. of sulphur. It also contains a large proportion of oil. The use of sulphur in promoting the growth of the hair is well known. Its *modus operandi* in so doing is a matter about which there is great difference of opinion. Some physicians think it acts simply as an irritant; while others think that it acts by furnishing sulphur to the hair follicles. Both views of its action are simply theories, and are given here for what they are worth.

### ARTERIES.

A deposit of calcareous matter occasionally occurs in the coats of the arteries, especially the middle coat. It is, according to Rindfleisch (*Pathological Histology, p.* 215), purely a calcareous deposit; this observer has never detected anything "which answered to the anatomical dignity of a bone corpuscle." If it depends upon a co-existing osteo-malacia, which Green (*Pathology and Morbid Anatomy, pp.* 74–75,) says is a common cause of the disease, the mineral acids can not be used, but if it were from a superabundance of calcareous salts in the blood, without structural change of bone, the mineral acids, particularly hydrochloric, would seem to be indicated.

### FAECES.

Chemical examination of the faeces has been very much neglected by both physiologists and pathologists; and yet there is no subject which is more worthy of study, or a knowledge of whose chemical composition would better repay the practical physician. The vicarious elimination of urea and some other excrementitious principles by the alimentary canal, have already been spoken of; and we have also briefly considered the fatty diarrhœa, which is probably indicative of disease of the pancreas, and for the relief of which pancreatine is used. With our present ignorance concerning the physiology of the fæces, but little more can be said about the information to be derived from it relative to pathology. We have no doubt, however, that the time will soon come when fecal pathology will occupy as prominent a position as urinary pathology now does.

---

## PART III.

### POISONS.

A thorough knowledge of the chemical relations of the different poisons is of great service in the practice of medicine ; but the tests for the various poisons, while it is a subject of the greatest moment, on which often hang the issues of life and death, are not generally made by the medical practitioner, but by chemical experts. For this reason we do not think it necessary to consider the tests for poisons in this paper. Galloway's "Manual of Qualitative Chemical Analysis" describes the tests for the various poisons very fully, and yet presents them in a form which is easy of execution. The antidotes for the different poisons it is of vital importance for every physician to know, and it shall now be our aim to point out the chemical antidotes for the different poisons to the best of our ability. The following table, taken for the most part from Taylor on Poisons, pp. 75–76, gives a tolerably full list of the poisons and their antidotes, so far as those antidotes act chemically. With the physiological antidotes of the poisons we have nothing to do:

### POISONS—ANTIDOTES.

ACIDS.—The antidotes for acids are the alkalies, generally ; magnesia, carbonate of lime, chalk, carbonate of soda or of potash. For oxalic and tartaric acids carbonate of lime is the best antidote.

BINOXALATE AND BITARTRATE OF POTASH.—The carbonates of lime and soda or sulphate of lime dissolved in water.

ALKALIES.—Vinegar, lemon juice, citric acid and oil.

BARYTA AND ITS SOLUBLE SALTS.—Sulphates of soda, potash, magnesia or lime.

ALUM.—Carbonate of soda, or sesqui-carbonate of ammonia.

ARSENIC.—Hydrated sesquioxide of iron, hydrated magnesia.

MERCURY.—Albumen in some form : the white of egg.

LEAD.—The alkaline sulphates, dilute sulphuric acid.

CARBONATE LEAD.—Sulphate of magnesia and vinegar diluted. First forms acetate of lead which is neutralized by the sulphate magnesia.

COPPER.—Albumen from eggs, milk, gluten or flour stirred in water.

TARTARIZED ANTIMONY.—Tannic acid, or substances containing it, and magnesia.

CHLORIDE OF ANTIMONY.—Carbonate of soda and magnesia.

TIN AND ZINC.—Milk, carbonate of soda, and magnesia.— (*Taylor*). Orfila says that tin is not poisonous.—(*Mialhe, p.* 368).

SULPHATE IRON.—Carbonate of soda and sesqui-carbonate of ammonia.

NITRATE OF SILVER.—Chloride of sodium or common salt. Forms by double decomposition nitrate of soda and chloride of silver.

Iodine has been proposed as an antidote to strychnine, but I know of no case in which it has been used. It is incompatible with the strychnine and quinine, and probably other vegetable alkaloids, and for this reason was proposed as an antidote to strychnine.

## PART IV.

### CHEMICAL INCOMPATIBLES.

The subject of chemical incompatibles is according to Parrish (*Practical Pharmacy*, *p.* 456) too much of a stumbling block to the student. We think he underrates the importance of the subject. It is only necessary for one to inquire of a druggist who is in the habit of filling prescriptions, to learn how frequently mistakes of this character occur. For example, a prescription, which is not very unusual, is one composed of oxalate of cerium and lime water. The lime water decomposes the oxalate of cerium and oxalate of lime is formed, which, as we have seen, constitutes one form of calculus. It is true that it is very insoluble but, we do not think any thinking man in the present state of our knowledge would like to administer oxalate of lime. On the other hand physicians are sometimes prevented from combining medicines which are perfectly compatible because they think them incompatible. A few days ago we heard a gentleman wish that he could combine bromide of sodium and chloral hydrate in the same prescription, but he said he was confident they would decompose each other. We knew nothing to the contrary, but on general principles did not think they were incompatible. A trial proved them to be perfectly compatible chemically.

I have determined, therefore, to devote some space to the consideration of this subject, although it is one about which, more than any other, I feel my own *great* ignorance. To give a complete list of incompatibles or even the action upon each other of the *very various* ingredients of the prescriptions of some physicians, who seem to think that " there is safety in numbers," would require a volume as large as Webster's dictionary (unabridged.)

In the following very incomplete list taken for the most part from Dunglison's " Therapeutics and Materia Medica," I shall endeavor to give the most prominent incompatibles :

Acidum Arseniosum, Arsenious Acid.—Bark, decoction of. Copper, sulphate of. Lime water. Silver, nitrate of. Potassium, iodide of. Potassa, sulphohydrate of.

Acidum Hydrocyanicum, Hydrocyanic Acid.—Acids, mineral. Antimony, oxides of. Chlorine. Iron, salts of. Mercury, oxides of. Oxides generally. Silver, nitrate of. Sulphurets.

Acidum Muriaticum, Muriatic Acid.—Alkalies. Carbonates. Earths. Lead, acetate of. Oxides. Potassa, sulphate of. Potassa, tartrate of. Silver, nitrate of.

Acidum Nitricum, Nitric Acid.—Alcohol. Alkalies. Carbonates. Earths. Iron, protosulphate of. Lead, acetate of. Oils, essential. Oxides. Potassa, acete of. Sulphurets. Zinc, sulphate of.　　　　•

Acidum Oxalicum, Oxalic Acid.—Lime, salts of.

Acidum Sulphuricum, Sulphuric Acid.—Alcohol. Barium, chloride of. Calcium, chloride of. Carbonates. Chlorohydrates. Nitrates. Oils, essential. Organic substances. Oxides. Sulphohydrates. Vegetable astringent infusions.

Acidum Tartaricum, Tartaric Acid.—Alkalies. Carbonates, alkaline. Carbonates, earthy. Earths. Lead, salts of. Lime, salts of. Lime water, Mercury, salts of. Potassa, salts of. Vegetable astringents.

Alumen, Alum.—Alkalies. Alkaline salts. Ammonia, carbonate of. Ammonia, chlorohydrate of. Galls. Kino. Lead, acetate of. Lime water. Magnesia, carbonate of. Mercury, salts of. Potassa, tartrate of

Ammoniæ Acetatis Liquor, Solution of Acetate of Ammonia.—Acids. Alkalies. Alum. Copper, sulphate of. Iron, sulphate of. Lime water. Lead, acetate of. Magnesia, sulphate of. Mercury, bichloride of. Silver, nitrate of. Zinc, sulphate of.

Ammoniæ Liquor, Solution of Ammonia.—Acids. Alum, Salts, metallic.

Ammoniæ Carbonas, Carbonate of Ammonia.—Acids. Alkalies, fixed. Alum. Carbonates, alkaline. Iron, sulphate of. Lead, acetate of. Lime. Lime, chloride of. Magnesia. Magnesia, sulphate of. Mercury, acetate of. Mercury, bichloride of. Mercury, protochloride of. Potassa, bitartrate of. Salts, acidulous. Zinc, sulphate of.

Ammoniæ Murias, Muriate of Ammonia.—Acid, sulphuric. Acid, nitric. Alkalies, fixed. Carbonates, alkaline. Iron, sulphate of. Lead, acetate of. Lime. Magnesia. Magnesia, sulphate of. Potassa. Potassa, carbonate of. Salts, metallic. Silver, nitrate of. Zinc, sulphate of.

Antimonii et Potassæ Tartras, Tartrate of Antimony and Potassa.—Acids, mineral. Alkalies. Carbonates, alkaline. Decoctions, bitter. Earths. Sulphohydrates. Infusions, bitter. Metals. Soaps.

Argenti Nitras, Nitrate of Silver.—Acid, arsenious. Acid, chlorohydric and salts. Acid, sulphuric and salts. Acid, tartaric and salts. Alkalies, fixed. Earths, alkaline. Sulphohydrates. Soaps. Vegetable astringent infusions. Water, common.

Calcis Liquor, Lime Water.—Acids. Borates. Citrates. Infusions, astringent. Salts, alkaline. Salts, metallic. Sulphur. Tartrates. Tinctures. Oxalates

Cupri Sulphas, SULPHATE OF COPPER.—Alkalies. Ammonia, acetate of. Calcium, chloride of. Carbonates, alkaline. Lead, acetate of. Lead, triacetate of. Lime water. Mercury, bichloride of. Potassa, tartrate of. Silver, nitrate of. Soda, biborate of. Vegetable astringent infusions. Vegetable astringent tinctures.

Ferri Chloridi Tinctura, TINCTURE OF CHLORIDE OF IRON.—Alkalies. Carbonates, alkaline. Mucilage. Vegetable astringent infusions.

Ferri et Potassæ Tartras, TARTRATE OF IRON AND POTASSA.—Acids Lime water. Potassa, sulphohydrate of. Vegetable astringents infusions.

Ferri Sulphas, SULPHATE OF IRON.—Alkalies. Ammonia, acetate of. Ammonia, chlorohydrate of. Carbonates, alkaline. Earths. Lead, acetate of. Lead, triacetate of. Potassa, nitrate of. Potasse and soda, tartrate of. Salts, with base forming insoluble sulphates. Silver, nitrate of. Soda. Soda, biborate of. Vegetable astringent infusions.

Hydrargyri Chloridum Corrosivum, CORROSIVE CHLORIDE OF MERCURY.—Almond mixture. Alkalies, fixed. Ammonia. Antimony and potassa, tartrate of. Bismuth. Carbonates, alkaline. Copper. Iron. Lead. Lead, acetate of. Lime water. Mercury. Oils, volatile. Potassium, sulphuret of. Silver, nitrate of. Soap. Sulphur. Zinc. Chamomile, infusions of. Cinchona, infusions of. Columbo, infusions of. Horseradish, infusions of. Oak bark, infusions of. Senna, infusions of. Simaruba, infusions of. Tea, infusions of.

Hydrargyi Chloridum Mite, MILD CHLORIDE OF MERCURY.—Acid, nitric. Alkalies. Antimony, golden sulphuret of. Carbonates, alkaline. Chlorine. Copper. Iron. Lead. Lime water. Potassium, sulphuret of. Soaps.

Liquor Arsenici et Hydrargyri, SOLUTION OF ARSENIC AND MERCURY.—Laudnum. Sulphate, muriate and acetate of Morphia.

Lupulina., LUPULINE.—Iron. Mercury, salts of. Platinum, salts of. Tin, salts of.

Magnesiæ Carbonas, CARBONATE OF MAGNESIA.—Acids. Alkalies. Alum. Copper, sulphate of. Iron, sulphate of. Lead, acetate of. Mercury, bichloride of. Potassa, bitartrate of. Salts, acidulous. Salts, neutral. Silver, nitrate of. Zinc, sulphate of.

Magnesiæ Sulphas, SULPHATE OF MAGNESIA.—Alkalies, fixed. Ammonia, muriate of. Barium, chloride of. Calcium, chloride of. Carbonates, alkaline. Lead, acetates of. Silver, nitrate of.

Morphia, MORPHIA.—Oxides, metallic.

Morphia, Salts of.—Alkalies. Carbonates, alkaline. Decoctions of vegetable astringents. Infusions of vegetable astringents. Lime. Magnesia. Silver, nitrate of.

Opium (solid), OPIUM —Alkalies. Cinchona. Galls. Lead, acetate of. Mercury, bichloride of.

Plumbi Acetas, ACETATE OF LEAD.—Acids. Alkalies. Alum. Ammonia, solution of acetate of. Antimony and potassa, tartrate of. Carbonates, alkaline. Earths, alkaline. Cholorohydrates. Iron, ammoniated. Iron and potassa, tartrate of. Soaps. Soda, biborate of. Sulphates. Sulphurets. Water, common.

Plumbi Subacetatis Liquor, SOLUTION OF SUBACETATE OF LEAD.—Alkalics. Carbonates, alkaline. Mucilage. Soap liniment. Sulphates, alkaline. Sulphurets of alkaline metals.

Potassæ Acetas, ACETATE OF POTASSA.—Fruits, acid.   Acid, mineral. Tamarinds. Salts, acid. Salts, alkaline. Salts, metallic.

Potassæ Arsentis Liquor, SOLUTION OF ARSENITE OF POTASSA.—Cinchona, infusion of. Copper, salts of. Lime water. Potassa, sulphohydrate of. Silver, nitrate of.

Potassæ Carbonas, CARBONATE OF POTASSA.—See Potassæ bicarbonas.

Potassæ Bicarbonas, BICARBONATE OF POTASSA.—Acids. Alum. Ammonia, acetate of. Ammonia, carbonate of. Ammonia, muriate of. Antimony and potassa, tartrate of. Copper, acetate of. Copper, sulphate of. Iron, chloride of. Iron and potassa, tartrate of. Iron, sulphate of. Lead, acetate of. Lime water. Magnesia, sulphate of. Mercury, bichloride of. Mercury, protochloride of. Silver, nitrate of. Salts, acidulus. Soda, biborate of. Zince, sulphate of.

Potassæ Nitras, NITRATE OF POTASSA —Acid, sulphuric. Alum. Copper, sulphate of. Iron, sulphate of. Magnesia, sulphate of. Soda, sulphate of. Zinc, sulphate of.

Potassæ Sulphas, SULPHATE OF POTASSA.—Acid, chlorohydric. Acid, nitric. Lead, acetate of. Lime and compounds. Mercury, bichloride of. Silver, nitrate of.

Posassæ Tartras, TARTRATE OF POTASSA.—Acids. Barium, chloride of. Lead, acetates of. Lime. Magnesia, Salts, acidulous. Silver, nitrate of. Tamarinds. Vegetables, acid.

Potassæ Bitartras, BITARTRATE OF POTASSA.—Acids, mineral. Alkalies. Earths, alkaline.

Quiniæ Sulphas, SULPHATE OF QUINIA.—Alkalies. Earths, alkaline. Infusion of orange-peel, compound. Infusion of Roses. Solutions, astringent. Tincture of cinchona. Iodine.

Sodæ Boras, BORATE OF SODA.—Acids. Ammonia, chlorohydrate of. Ammonia, sulphate of. Chlorohydrates, earthy. Potassa. Sulphates, earthy.

Sodæ Carbenas, CARBONATE OF SODA.—See Carbonate of Potash.

Sodæ et Potassæ Tartras, TARTRATE OF SODA AND POTASSA.—Acids. Ammonia, muriate of. Baryta, salts of. Lead, acetate of. Lime, salts of. Magnesia, sulphate of. Potassa, sulphate of. Salts, acidulous. Soda, sulphate of. Tamarinds.

Sodæ Sulphas, SULPHATE OF SODA —Acid, chlorohydric. Acid, nitric. Acid, sulphuric. Barium, chloride of. Lime. Magnesia.

Sodæ Sulphas, SULPHATE OF SODA.—See Magnesia Sulphas.

Zinci Sulphas, SUPHATE OF ZINC.—Alkalies. Earths. Milk. Sulphohydrates. Vegetable astringent infusions.

---

In this essay, which I am now about to bring to an end, it has been my aim as far as possible to confine myself to subjects which were well understood, and when I have given theories which had not been proven, I have generally stated that they were *only* theories. I have endeavored, too, to confine myself to those subjects a knowledge of which are of use to the physician in his daily life and practice; and when I have ventured to touch upon subjects which are as yet of purely scientific interest, it has been from the conviction that further investigations would show their *practical* import. The vast strides which organic chemistry is now making will undoubtedly throw great light on many points in medicine which are now very obscure.

There has been a tendency, we think, on the part of many of our ablest physicians to neglect chemistry, from an idea that viewing the changes which occur in disease as chemical changes tended to materialism ; and whole volumes have been written on the *vital* theory of disease. We are far from denying that there are *vital* changes as well as chemical changes in disease. In the present state of pathology the former are probably more prominent and important than the latter ; but we can see nothing in the chemical theory which militates against the Bible. Tyndall himself is no firmer believer in an universal " Reign of Law," than the writer of this article ; but until he can prove that there are no more laws undiscovered, and until he can foretell the effect produced by every possible combination, of known laws, I shall still believe that I have "a reason for the *faith* that is in me." Then—

> " Let knowledge grow from more to more,
> But more of reverence in us dwell .
> That mind and soul according well,
> May make one music as before,—
>
> But vaster."

www.ingramcontent.com/pod-product-compliance
Lightning Source LLC
Chambersburg PA
CBHW021638270326
41931CB00008B/1070

* 9 7 8 3 3 3 7 8 1 6 3 5 3 *